W9-BFM-665

ITALIAN FARMHOUSE COOKING

CHARTWELL
BOOKS, INC.

Published by Chartwell Books
a division of Book Sales, Inc.
114 Northfield Avenue
Edison, NJ 08837

This edition is produced for sale
in the U.S.A., its territories
and dependencies only.

Copyright © 1994 Parragon Book Service Ltd
Copyright © in design 1994 Haldane Mason

ISBN 0-7858-0421-8

Edited, designed and typeset by Haldane Mason
Editor: Joanna Swinnerton

Note: Cup measurements in this book are for standard American cups. Unless otherwise stated, milk is assumed to be full-fat, and pepper is freshly ground black pepper. All butter is sweet unless otherwise stated.

CONTENTS

FRESH TOMATO SAUCE
SALSA AL POMODORO

This sauce is worth the effort. To peel the tomatoes, prick them all over with the tip of a pointed knife, cover with boiling water for 10 minutes, rinse, and place in cold water. The skins should then come off easily.

MAKES 5 cups
4 tbsp olive oil
6 shallots or 1 large onion, sliced
4 garlic cloves, crushed
14 oz can tomatoes
1 lb fresh ripe tomatoes
4 tbsp chopped parsley
2½ cups hot vegetable stock
1 tbsp sugar
2 tbsp lemon juice
⅔ cup dry white wine
salt and pepper

1 Heat the oil in a large pan. Add the shallots and garlic, and fry for about 3 minutes until they start to soften.

2 Add the canned and fresh tomatoes, parsley, stock, sugar, and lemon juice. Bring to the boil and stir well. Cover the pan and simmer for 15 minutes.

3 Stir in the wine and season to taste. You may need to add a little more sugar if the tomatoes are quite acidic.

4 Use as required, or reduce to a more concentrated sauce by simmering for longer.

This sauce keeps well for about 5 days if refrigerated, and can be frozen. It is best frozen in its more concentrated form and in small quantities for easy defrosting.

Fresh Tomato Sauce

WHITE SAUCE
BESCIAMELLA

This is a good all-purpose sauce that can be used in meat, fish, and vegetable dishes. Use a selection of gently aromatic vegetables, avoiding any that might taint the color of the sauce.

MAKES 2¹/₂ cups

cups milk

1 shallot or onion, halved

1 carrot, quartered

1 celery stalk, chopped roughly

1 bay leaf

several peppercorns

¹/₄ cup butter

¹/₂ cup all-purpose flour

grated nutmeg

2 egg yolks, beaten, or ²/₃ cup heavy cream (optional)

salt and white pepper

1 Place the milk, shallot, carrot, celery, bay leaf, and peppercorns in a pan and bring to the boil. Remove from the heat and leave to infuse for 30–60 minutes.

2 Melt the butter in a large pan and stir in the flour. Remove from the heat and gradually whisk in the strained, flavored milk.

3 Return to the heat, stirring constantly until the sauce thickens, taking care not to let it 'catch' and burn on the bottom of the pan. Allow to cool slightly, then season with a pinch of grated nutmeg, and salt and pepper to taste.

For a richer sauce, whisk in the egg yolks or the heavy cream as required.

This sauce will keep chilled for up to a week, or can be frozen in useful quantities.

TUSCAN BEAN SOUP
ZUPPA DI FAGIOLI ALLA FIORENTINA

If you are using dried borlotti beans, soak the beans overnight in water, then boil rapidly in fresh water for 10 minutes. Drain and rinse, then boil again in fresh water for 5 minutes.

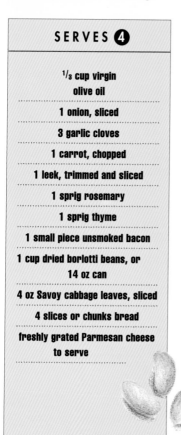

SERVES 4

¹/₃ cup virgin olive oil

1 onion, sliced

3 garlic cloves

1 carrot, chopped

1 leek, trimmed and sliced

1 sprig rosemary

1 sprig thyme

1 small piece unsmoked bacon

1 cup dried borlotti beans, or 14 oz can

4 oz Savoy cabbage leaves, sliced

4 slices or chunks bread

freshly grated Parmesan cheese to serve

1 Crush 2 of the garlic cloves. Heat the oil in a large pan and fry the onion and crushed garlic until softened but not brown. Add the carrot, leek, herbs, bacon, and the dried borlotti beans, if using.

2 Stir in 3¹/₂ cups water and simmer the mixture for about 1 hour, until the beans are tender.

3 Remove the piece of bacon and set aside. Using a perforated spoon, remove half of the beans and press them through a strainer or purée by working in a blender. Stir the bean purée into the soup with the cabbage and simmer for 10 minutes. If you are using canned beans, drain, then purée half of them and stir them into the soup with the remaining whole beans and cabbage.

4 Cut the remaining clove of garlic in half. Toast the bread and rub it on both sides with the cut side of the garlic. Place the bread in the bottom of a soup tureen. Pour the soup over the bread and serve with Parmesan cheese.

8

The boiled bacon is not wasted, as it can be served cold with bread and pickles as a separate meal.

9

MINESTRONE SOUP

MINESTRONE

Use half the quantity of Fresh Tomato Sauce on page 4 as the base for this soup. Italian unsmoked bacon is traditionally used in this recipe, but other unsmoked bacon or belly pork may be used as a substitute.

SERVES 4

¹/₄ cup diced Italian unsmoked bacon

1 carrot, sliced

1 celery stalk, sliced

1 zucchini, sliced

2 potatoes, diced

3¹/₂ cups vegetable stock

¹/₂ quantity Fresh Tomato Sauce (see page 4)

15 oz can cannellini beans

1 sprig fresh sage, chopped

1 tbsp chopped fresh basil

³/₄ cup peas

¹/₃ cup stelline or tiny pasta shapes

salt and pepper

---

1 Fry the Italian unsmoked bacon in its own fat over a low heat. Add the carrot, celery, zucchini, and potatoes and fry gently for 10 minutes.

2 Stir in the vegetable stock, fresh tomato sauce, drained canned beans, and herbs and simmer for 5 minutes. Season to taste.

3 Add the peas and pasta, and simmer the soup for a further 10 minutes, or until the vegetables and pasta are tender.

4 Divide the soup between 4 soup bowls and serve immediately with grated Parmesan cheese, and perhaps some chunks of warmed Italian bread.

10

PRESERVED MEATS
SALUMI

SERVES 4

2 oz Italian salami, sliced thinly

4 thin slices mortadella

6 slices prosciutto

6 slices bresaola

3 ripe tomatoes, sliced thinly

4 fresh basil leaves, chopped

olive oil

3 ripe figs, quartered

1 small melon, cut into wedges

1/2 cup marinated pitted olives

pepper to serve

Salumi are preserved meats and are often served as a first course. Mix an attractive selection of these meats with olives and marinated vegetables for extra color and variety.

1 Choose a selection of Italian meats according to your preference. The following are some of the most common. Prosciutto is a fine quality raw ham that is rubbed with salt, sugar, and spices before being matured. Italian salami comes in many varieties, but is usually made of beef, pork, and pork fat flavored with garlic and pepper. Mortadella is one of the largest sausages and consists of pork, garlic, and seasoning, and sometimes pistachio nuts or coriander seeds. Bresaola is dried salt beef, and is served in very thin slices.

2 Arrange the meats on one half of a serving platter. Arrange the tomato slices in the center, and sprinkle with the basil leaves and oil.

3 Cover the rest of the platter with the fruit and scatter the olives over the meats.

Serve with a little extra olive oil to drizzle over the bresaola, and a peppermill filled with black peppercorns.

12

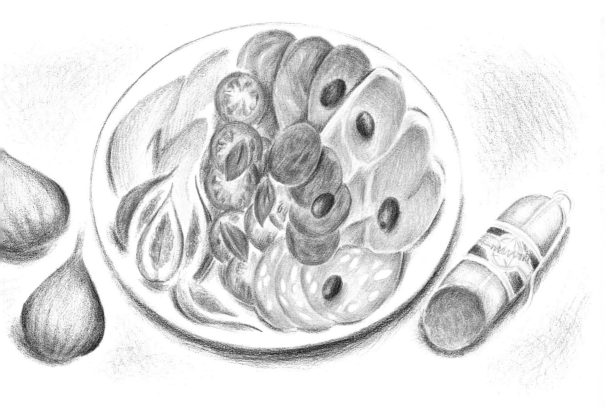

GARLIC BREAD WITH TOMATOES

BRUSCHETTA AL POMODORO

***These delicious snacks can be turned into mini pizzas
simply by adding Mozzarella cheese.***

SERVES 4

1 lb fresh ripe tomatoes, peeled

4 tbsp olive oil

4 fresh basil leaves, chopped

1 tsp chopped fresh marjoram
leaves

4 thick slices crusty bread,
lightly toasted

2 garlic cloves

¾ cup diced Mozzarella cheese,
(optional)

salt and pepper

1 Halve the tomatoes and remove and discard the seeds. Dice the flesh, and mix with the oil and herbs.

2 Cut each garlic clove in half and rub over both sides of each slice of bread to flavor them. (This is easier if you spear the garlic clove on a fork.)

3 Arrange the tomato mixture on top of the bread, add the Mozzarella cheese if using, and season to taste. Place under a preheated moderate broiler until warmed through, or until the cheese has melted. Take care not to burn the bread – the edges tend to burn quite easily.

Garlic Bread with Tomatoes

15

BLACK OLIVE PATE
PATE DI OLIVE NERE

This pâté is delicious mixed with hot spaghetti and tuna fish; use about 3 tbsp for 1 lb cooked pasta, add a small can of drained tuna and a dash of cream for a quick meal. It can also be served as a cocktail snack, on small circles of fried bread.

MAKES 1 1/2 cups

1 1/2 cups pitted juicy black olives

1 garlic clove, crushed

finely grated rind of 1 lemon

4 tbsp lemon juice

1/2 cup fresh breadcrumbs

1/4 cup cream cheese

salt and pepper

1 Put all the ingredients except the salt and pepper in a mixing bowl, and pound until smooth, or place in a food processor and work until fully blended. Season to taste with salt and freshly ground black pepper.

2 Store in a screwtop jar and chill for several hours before using – this allows the flavors to develop.

For a delicious cocktail snack, use a pastry cutter to cut out small circles of bread from a thickly sliced loaf, and fry them in a mixture of olive oil and butter until they are a light golden brown. Top each round with a little of the pâté, garnish with tiny pieces of tomato, and serve them immediately with ice-cold Frascati wine.

This pâté will keep chilled in an airtight jar for up to 2 weeks.

Black Olive Pâté

FISH SOUP
ZUPPA DI PESCE

Any mixture of white fish, such as cod, hake, or haddock, can be used in this dish. Take great care not to touch your eyes or lips while preparing the chili, and wash your hands thoroughly after handling it, as the bitter juices will remain on your skin.

SERVES 6

2 lb mussels, scrubbed and bearded

1 lb clams, scrubbed

4 tbsp olive oil

2 garlic cloves, crushed

1 small red chili, cored and deseeded

$\frac{1}{2}$ quantity Fresh Tomato Sauce (see page 4)

1 lb cod, hake, or haddock fillet, skinned

$\frac{2}{3}$ cup dry white wine

$1\frac{1}{4}$ cups hot fish stock made from bouillon cubes

salt and pepper

3 tbsp chopped parsley to garnish

1 Put the mussels and clams in a large pan with about 2 inches water. Cover the pan and bring to the boil. Steam the shellfish for about 5 minutes, shaking the pan frequently.

2 Discard any shellfish that have not opened. Rinse in cold water to remove any grit and reserve. Rinse the pan and heat the oil in it. Add the garlic and chili, and fry for 2 minutes. Add the fresh tomato sauce, white fish, and wine. Simmer over a low heat for about 10 minutes, until the fish is cooked.

3 Remove the chili. Cool the mixture for 10 minutes, then rub it through a strainer or purée in a blender until smooth.

4 Return to the pan and stir in the fish stock. Add the steamed shellfish, and heat through. Season to taste.

Serve, sprinkled with parsley, with crusty bread.

Fish Soup

HOMEMADE PASTA WITH TOMATO SAUCE

PASTA AL POMODORO

Pasta is easy to make and can be made in a food processor to save time. This recipe is for Pasta Verde, so leave out the spinach to make plain egg pasta.

SERVES 6

8 oz fresh spinach, washed

4 cups all-purpose flour

pinch of salt

3 eggs, beaten

1 tbsp olive oil

1 quantity Fresh Tomato Sauce (see page 4)

grated Parmesan or Pecorino cheese to serve

1 Drain the spinach well. Place in a pan, cover, and cook over a low heat without any extra liquid until soft, about 8 minutes. Transfer to a strainer and press out as much juice as possible. Rub through a strainer or purée in a blender.

2 Combine the spinach purée, flour, salt, eggs, and oil, or work in a food processor, until the mixture holds together. Knead on a lightly floured counter until smooth and elastic. Cut the dough in half, wrap in plastic wrap and leave to rest for 30 minutes.

3 On a lightly floured counter roll out each piece of dough from the center out, until it is as thin as possible without tearing. Leave to rest for 10 minutes, then cut into narrow strips.

4 Heat the fresh tomato sauce and keep warm. Bring a large pan of salted water to the boil and add a little oil. Add the

20

pasta, bring back to the boil and cook for 5 minutes or until *al dente* – firm to the bite.

5 Drain the pasta well and transfer to a warmed serving dish. Pour the fresh tomato sauce over it and serve with the Parmesan or Pecorino cheese.

SPINACH AND RICOTTA GNOCCHI

GNOCCHI DI RICOTTA

Try not to handle the mixture too much when making gnocchi, as this will make the dough a little heavy.

SERVES ❹

- **2 lb spinach, washed**
- **1¹/₂ cups Ricotta cheese**
- **1 cup Pecorino cheese, grated**
- **3 eggs, beaten**
- **¹/₄ tsp freshly grated nutmeg**
- **all-purpose flour**
- **¹/₂ cup butter**
- **¹/₄ cup pine nuts**
- **¹/₃ cup raisins**
- **salt and pepper**

1 Drain the spinach well and cook in a covered pan without any extra liquid until softened, about 8 minutes. Place in a colander and press well to remove as much juice as possible. Either rub the spinach through a strainer or purée in a blender.

2 Combine the spinach purée with the Ricotta cheese, half the Pecorino cheese, the eggs, grated nutmeg, and seasoning to taste, mixing lightly but thoroughly. Work in enough flour, lightly and quickly, to make the mixture easy to handle.

3 Shape the pasta dough quickly into small lozenge shapes, and dust lightly with flour.

4 Add a dash of oil to a large pan of salted water and bring to the boil. Add the gnocchi carefully and boil for about 2 minutes until they float on the top. Use a perforated spoon and transfer to a buttered ovenproof dish. Keep warm.

5 Melt the butter in a skillet, add the nuts and raisins, and fry until the nuts start to brown

Spinach and Ricotta Gnocchi

slightly, but do not allow the butter to burn. Pour this mixture over the gnocchi

and serve sprinkled with the remaining Pecorino cheese.

23

PASTA WITH PESTO
PASTA AL PESTO

This rich, heady sauce is the essence of an Italian summer. Thin it down with a little extra oil and drizzle it over seafood or mix with pasta. One delicious way to use it is to smear it over halved tomatoes, sprinkle them with Parmesan, and bake. These quantities make more than enough pesto for this recipe; the rest will keep for up to a week in the refrigerator in a sealed container.

SERVES ❹

1–1¹/₂ cups fresh basil

2 large garlic cloves, peeled

³/₄ cup pine nuts

4 tbsp grated Pecorino or Parmesan cheese

2 tbsp lemon juice

²/₃ cup olive oil

12 oz fresh fettuccine

salt and pepper

freshly grated Parmesan cheese to serve (optional)

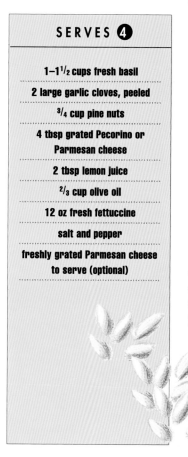

1 Put the basil leaves, garlic, pine nuts, cheese, lemon juice, and half the oil in a mortar and pound with a pestle, or work in a food processor until smooth. Add enough of the remaining olive oil to make a soft paste. Season to taste.

2 Bring a large pan of salted water to the boil and add a dash of oil. Add the fettuccine and bring back to the boil. Stir well, then cook for about 5 minutes, or until *al dente* – firm to the bite. Fresh pasta cooks much more quickly than dried pasta, so watch it carefully and stir occasionally to prevent it from sticking together.

3 Drain the fettuccine and return to the pan. Add enough of the basil sauce to coat well. Serve immediately with grated Parmesan if liked.

LINGUINE WITH WALNUTS
LINGUINE CON LE NOCCI

This rich nut sauce can be served with any kind of pasta and can also be used as a filling for ravioli.
This recipe makes enough walnut paste for this dish, with plenty left over.

SERVES 4

3 cups shelled walnuts

1/2 cup fresh white breadcrumbs

4 tbsp milk

2 garlic cloves, crushed

4 tbsp virgin olive oil

1/3 cup cream cheese

12 oz dried linguine

2/3 cup light cream (optional)

salt and pepper

freshly grated Parmesan cheese to serve

---

1 Put the walnuts, breadcrumbs, milk, garlic, olive oil, and cream cheese in a mortar and pound with a pestle until smooth, or work in a food processor. Season to taste.

2 Bring a large pan of water to the boil with a dash of oil and a pinch of salt. When boiling, add the linguine and cook until *al dente* – firm to the bite.

3 Drain and return to the pan with 3/4 cup of the walnut paste and a little cream if using Toss well. Serve with freshly grated Parmesan.

The remaining walnut paste will keep well in the refrigerator in an airtight container for up to 2 weeks.

LASAGNE

LASAGNE VERDE ALLA BOLOGNESE

This seems a long-winded recipe, but it is worth making for a special occasion, as it outshines all the quick versions usually encountered in the name of lasagne. To save time, you can use dried lasagne sheets instead of making fresh pasta.

1 Grease a 2 quart deep ovenproof dish.

2 Finely chop the pork, steak, prosciutto, and chicken livers, and combine with the fresh tomato sauce, or put in a food processor and work until the meat is finely chopped.

3 Transfer to a pan and stir in the cream. Simmer gently for 30 minutes until the meat is cooked, adding a little water if necessary to prevent it from drying out.

4 Heat the oil in a skillet and fry the bacon for 10 minutes.

Add to the meat sauce and season to taste.

5 If using fresh pasta, roll out the pasta thinly and cut into 6 strips wide enough for 2 strips to cover the base of the dish. Bring a large pan of salted water to the boil and add a dash of oil. Cook 2 pasta strips at a time for about 2 minutes, carefully lift out, and cook the remaining strips in the same way. If you are using dried pasta, cook as directed on the packet.

6 Place 2 strips in the base of the dish and cover with a

layer of meat sauce, then a layer of white sauce, and a third of the Parmesan cheese. Repeat twice.

7 Place in a preheated oven at 350°F, and bake for 30–40 minutes. Allow to stand for 10 minutes before serving.

SAUSAGES WITH LENTILS
SALSICCHIA CON LENTICCHE

The sausages can be cooked separately, but if they are baked on top of the lentils, as in this recipe, it gives the lentils a lot of extra flavor. Use other spicy sausages if you can't get the Luganega sausages.

SERVES 4

1¼ cups Puy lentils, rinsed thoroughly

¼ cup diced Italian unsmoked bacon

1 large onion, sliced

2 garlic cloves, chopped

2 celery stalks, sliced

1 parsnip, diced

1 tsp fresh rosemary leaves

⅔ cup dry white wine

1¼ cups hot vegetable stock

1 lb Italian Luganega pork sausages, pricked

salt and pepper

---

1 Put the rinsed lentils into a pan, cover with cold water, and bring to the boil. Boil rapidly for 10 minutes, then simmer for 20 minutes. Drain.

2 Place the Italian unsmoked bacon in a pan and cook over a low heat until the fat starts to run. Add the onion, garlic, celery, and parsnip and fry gently for 10 minutes. Stir in the rosemary, and season to taste. Add the wine and combine with the lentils and stock.

3 Transfer the mixture to a greased ovenproof dish and arrange the sausages on top. Cover the dish with foil, place in a preheated oven at 400°F, and bake for 25 minutes. Remove the foil and cook for a further 15 minutes until the sausages are cooked.

Serve with crusty bread to mop up the juices.

Sausages with Lentils

31

LAZY POLENTA WITH RABBIT STEW

POLENTA DI CONIGLIO

Polenta is an indispensable Italian dish, made from cornmeal. It can be served fresh, as in this dish, or it can be cooled, then sliced, and broiled.

SERVES ❹
generous 2 cups medium cornmeal
1 tbsp coarse sea salt
5 cups water
4 tbsp olive oil
4 lb rabbit pieces
3 garlic cloves, peeled
3 shallots, sliced
²/₃ cup red wine
1 carrot, sliced
1 celery stalk, sliced
2 bay leaves
1 sprig rosemary
3 tomatoes, peeled and diced
¹/₂ cup pitted black olives

1 Butter a large ovenproof dish. To make the polenta, mix the cornmeal, salt, and water in a large pan, whisking well. Bring to the boil and boil for 10 minutes. Turn into the buttered dish, place in a preheated oven at 375°F, and bake for 40 minutes.

2 Meanwhile, heat the oil in a large pan and add the rabbit pieces, garlic, and shallots. Fry for 10 minutes until browned. Stir in the wine and cook for a further 5 minutes.

3 Add the carrot, celery, bay leaves, rosemary, tomatoes, olives, and 1¹/₄ cups water. Cover the pan and simmer for about 45 minutes until the rabbit is tender. Season to taste.

To serve, spoon or cut a portion of polenta and place on each serving plate. Top with a ladleful of rabbit stew.

RICE AND PEAS
RISI E BISI

If you can get fresh peas (and willing helpers to shell them), do use them: you will need 2 lb.
Add them to the pan with the stock and continue with the recipe as written.

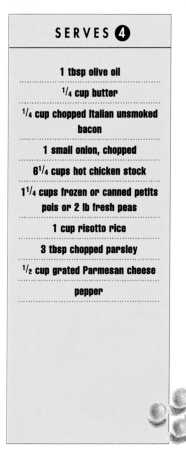

SERVES ❹

1 tbsp olive oil

¹/₄ cup butter

¹/₄ cup chopped Italian unsmoked bacon

1 small onion, chopped

6¹/₄ cups hot chicken stock

1¹/₄ cups frozen or canned petits pois or 2 lb fresh peas

1 cup risotto rice

3 tbsp chopped parsley

¹/₂ cup grated Parmesan cheese

pepper

1 Heat the oil and half the butter together. Add the Italian unsmoked bacon and onion and fry for 5 minutes. Add the stock and fresh peas if using and bring to the boil.

2 Stir in the rice and season to taste with pepper. Cook until the rice is tender, about 20–30 minutes, stirring occasionally.

3 Add the parsley and frozen or canned petits pois and cook for 8 minutes until the peas are thoroughly heated.

4 Stir in the remaining butter and the Parmesan cheese. Serve immediately, with freshly ground black pepper.

BEEF IN BAROLO
BRASATO AL BAROLO

Barolo is a famous wine from the Piedmont area of Italy. Its delicious, mellow flavor is the key to this dish, so don't stint on the quality of the wine.

SERVES 6

4 tbsp oil

2 lb piece boneless rolled rib of beef, or piece of round

2 garlic cloves, crushed

4 shallots, sliced

1 tsp fresh rosemary leaves

1 tsp fresh oregano leaves

2 celery stalks, sliced

1 large carrot, diced

2 whole cloves

1 bottle good Barolo wine

grated nutmeg

salt and pepper

1 Heat the oil in a flameproof casserole and brown the meat all over. Remove the meat from the casserole. Add the garlic, shallots, herbs, celery, carrot, and cloves and fry for 5 minutes.

2 Replace the meat on top of the vegetables. Pour in the wine. Cover the casserole and simmer gently for about 2 hours until tender. Remove the meat from the casserole, slice, and keep warm.

3 Rub the contents of the pan through a strainer or purée in a blender, adding a little hot beef stock if necessary. Season to taste with nutmeg, salt, and pepper.

Serve the meat with the sauce, accompanied by fresh spinach, carrots, and potatoes.

LAMB WITH OLIVES
AGNELLO CON OLIVE

SERVES 6

2¹/₂ lb boneless leg of lamb

¹/₃ cup olive oil

2 garlic cloves, crushed

1 onion, sliced

1 small red chili, cored, deseeded and chopped finely

³/₄ cup dry white wine

1 cup pitted black olives

salt

This is a very simple dish, and the chili gives it a kick. It is quick to prepare and makes an ideal supper dish. Take great care not to touch your eyes or lips while preparing the chili, and wash your hands thoroughly after handling it to remove the bitter juices.

1 Cut the lamb into cubes about 1 inch in size. Heat the oil in a skillet and fry the garlic, onion, and chili for 5 minutes. Add the wine and meat, and cook for a further 5 minutes. Stir in the olives.

2 Transfer the mixture to an ovenproof dish, place in a preheated oven at 350°F, and cook for about 1 hour 20 minutes until the meat is tender. Season to taste with salt. Serve with crusty bread, and cider or dry white wine to drink.

BARBECUED CHICKEN
POLLO ALLA DIAVOLA

SERVES ❹

3 lb chicken

grated rind of 1 lemon

4 tbsp lemon juice

2 sprigs rosemary

1 small red chili, chopped finely

²/₃ cup olive oil

You need a bit of brute force to prepare the chicken, but once marinated it's an easy and tasty candidate for the barbecue. Take great care not to touch your eyes or lips while preparing the chili, and wash your hands thoroughly after handling it to remove the bitter juices.

1 Split the chicken down the breast bone and open it out. Break the leg and wing joints to enable you to pound it flat. This ensures that it cooks evenly. Pound the chicken as flat as possible with a rolling pin.

2 Mix the lemon rind and juice, rosemary sprigs, chili, and olive oil together in a small bowl. Place the chicken in a large dish and pour over the marinade, turning the chicken to coat it evenly. Cover the dish and leave the chicken to marinate for at least 2 hours.

3 Cook the chicken over a hot barbecue (the coals should be white, and red when fanned) for about 30 minutes, turning it regularly until the skin is golden and crisp. To test if

it is cooked, pierce one of the
chicken thighs; if it is ready, the
juices should run clear, not pink.

Serve with a salad.

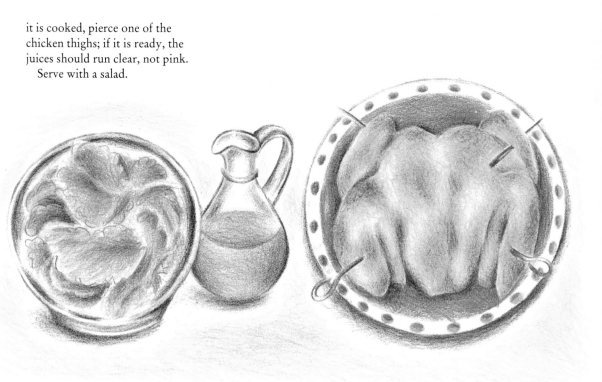

ROMAN CHICKEN
POLLO ALLA PEPERONE

This classic Roman dish makes an ideal light meal.
It is equally good cold and could be taken on a picnic —
serve with bread to mop up the juices.

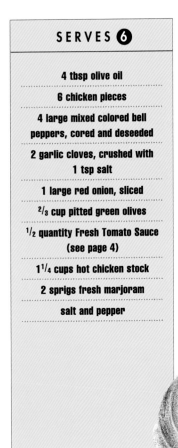

SERVES 6

4 tbsp olive oil

6 chicken pieces

4 large mixed colored bell
peppers, cored and deseeded

2 garlic cloves, crushed with
1 tsp salt

1 large red onion, sliced

²/₃ cup pitted green olives

¹/₂ quantity Fresh Tomato Sauce
(see page 4)

1¹/₄ cups hot chicken stock

2 sprigs fresh marjoram

salt and pepper

1 Heat half the oil in a flameproof casserole and brown the chicken pieces on all sides. Remove the chicken pieces and set aside.

2 Cut the bell peppers into strips. Add the remaining oil to the casserole and fry the garlic and onion until softened. Stir in the peppers, olives, and fresh tomato sauce.

3 Return the chicken to the casserole with the stock and marjoram. Cover the casserole and simmer for about 45 minutes until the chicken is tender. Season to taste with salt and pepper, and serve with crusty bread.

RUSTIC PIZZA
PIZZA RUSTICA

plain pastry dough for a 9-inch
double-crust pie

1¹/₂ cups Ricotta cheese

3 eggs, separated

¹/₄ cup diced salami

⅛ cup diced ham

2 tbsp grated Parmesan cheese

1 tsp fresh oregano leaves

1 large beefsteak tomato, sliced

6 oz Mozzarella cheese, sliced

3 oz smoked cheese, sliced

salt and pepper

*This is more like a pizza pie than a pizza, and is a real
slice of Italy to take on a summer picnic.
To save time, use 1 lb ready-made bread dough.*

1 Grease and flour a 9 inch loose-bottomed spring-form pan.

2 Roll out two-thirds of the pastry dough on a lightly floured counter, and use to line the base and sides of the pan.

3 Reserve 1 tbsp of the egg yolks and beat the remainder into the Ricotta cheese until smooth. Mix in the salami and ham.

4 Whisk the egg whites until stiff and fold into the mixture with the Parmesan cheese, and oregano. Season to taste. Spoon half the mixture into the pan and cover with the slices of tomato and Mozzarella cheese. Add the remaining mixture and cover with the slices of smoked cheese.

5 Brush the edge of the pastry with some of the reserved egg yolk. Roll out the remaining pastry and cover the pie. Crimp and seal the edges, brush the top

44

of the pie with the remaining egg yolk, and prick all over with a fork. Place in a preheated oven at 375°F, and bake for 45 minutes until golden. Cool in the pan for 10 minutes before serving.

BAKED FENNEL GRATIN
FINOCCHI GRATINATI

SERVES ❹

---

4 heads Florence fennel

2 tbsp butter

1 quantity White Sauce (see page 6), enriched with egg yolks

²/₃ cup dry white wine

¹/₂ cup fresh white breadcrumbs

3 tbsp grated Parmesan cheese

salt and pepper

Florence fennel, or finocchio is often used as a flavoring, but can also be served as a vegetable in its own right. In this dish its distinctive flavour is calmed by the smooth Besciamella.

1 Remove any bruised or tough outer stalks of fennel and cut each head in half.

2 Put into a pan of boiling salted water and simmer for 20 minutes or until tender. Drain the fennel.

3 Butter an ovenproof dish liberally and arrange the drained fennel in it. Mix the wine into the white sauce and season to taste. Pour over the fennel. Sprinkle evenly with the breadcrumbs and then the Parmesan cheese.

4 Place in a preheated oven at 400°F, and bake for 20 minutes until the top is golden.

46

Baked Fennel Gratin

BAKED EGGPLANT PARMA-STYLE

MELANZANE ALLA PARMIGIANA

Use the Fresh Tomato Sauce from the recipe on page 4 and simmer it gently to reduce it slightly before using.

SERVES 4

4 eggplants, trimmed

1 quantity reduced Fresh Tomato Sauce (see page 4)

3 tbsp olive oil

2 x 5 oz packets Mozzarella cheese, thinly sliced

4 slices prosciutto, shredded

1 tbsp chopped fresh marjoram leaves

1 tbsp chopped fresh basil

1/2 quantity White Sauce (see page 6)

1/4 cup grated Parmesan cheese

salt and pepper

1 Grease a shallow ovenproof dish.

2 Slice the eggplants thinly lengthwise. Bring a large pan of water to the boil and cook the eggplant slices for 5 minutes. Drain on paper towels and pat dry.

3 Pour half the fresh tomato sauce into the greased ovenproof dish. Cover with half the cooked eggplants and drizzle with a little oil.

Cover with half the Mozzarella cheese, prosciutto, and herbs. Season to taste. Repeat the layers and cover with the white sauce. Sprinkle with the Parmesan cheese, place in a preheated oven at 375°F, and bake for 35–40 minutes until golden on top.

ROAST BELL PEPPER SALAD
INSALATA DI PEPERONI ARROSTITI

This colorful salad can be served warm as a side dish, on toasted polenta or garlic bread. It is equally delicious served cold as an antipasto with cold meats.

SERVES 4

4 large mixed colored bell peppers

4 tbsp olive oil

1 large red onion, sliced

2 garlic cloves, crushed

4 tomatoes, peeled and chopped

pinch of sugar

1 tsp lemon juice

salt and pepper

1 Trim and halve the bell peppers and remove the seeds. Place skin-side up under a preheated hot broiler. Cook until the skins char. Rinse under cold water and remove the skins. Trim off any thick membranes and slice thinly.

2 Heat the oil and fry the onion and garlic until softened. Then add the bell peppers and tomatoes and fry over a low heat for 10 minutes. Remove from the heat, add the sugar and lemon juice, and season to taste.
Serve immediately, or leave to cool. The flavors will continue to develop as the salad cools.

Roast Bell Pepper Salad

FLAT BREAD
FOCACCIA

This delicious flat bread can be eaten on its own or cut into portions, slit, and stuffed with marinated vegetables, pepper salad, and cheeses. It is particularly good with a sprinkling of coarse sea salt on top, eaten with a rich olive or meat pâté.

SERVES 4

4 cups white bread flour

1 cake compressed yeast

4 tbsp warm water

pinch of sugar

6–8 tbsp olive oil

coarse sea salt

1 Put the flour in a large mixing bowl and make a well in the center. Blend the yeast with the water and sugar and leave until it froths.

2 Pour the yeast liquid and 2 tbsp of the oil into the well. Mix with enough warm water to make a soft dough.

3 Knead the dough on a lightly floured counter until it is smooth and elastic. Cover with greased baking parchment or oiled plastic wrap and leave to rise for 1 hour until it has doubled in size. Knead the dough again to punch down.

4 Pour half of the remaining oil (2–3 tbsp) into a shallow roasting pan and spread it evenly over the base. Put the dough in the pan and flatten it out into the corners to make it level. Pour the remaining oil (2–3 tbsp) over the top and smooth it over the dough with your fingertips. Push a finger into the dough to make dimples all over it and sprinkle the top with coarse sea salt.

5 Place in a preheated oven at 425°F, and bake for about 15–20 minutes until golden brown.

STUFFED PEACHES
PESCHE RIPIENE

Use ripe peaches for this recipe, so that they are really succulent when baked.

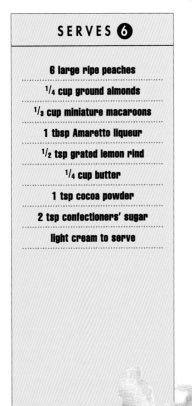

SERVES ❻

6 large ripe peaches

¹/₄ cup ground almonds

¹/₃ cup miniature macaroons

1 tbsp Amaretto liqueur

¹/₂ tsp grated lemon rind

¹/₄ cup butter

1 tsp cocoa powder

2 tsp confectioners' sugar

light cream to serve

1 Grease an ovenproof dish.

2 Halve the peaches and remove the pits. Scoop out a little of the flesh, leaving enough for the peach halves to hold their shape, and place the flesh in a mixing bowl.

3 Add the ground almonds, miniature macaroons, liqueur, lemon rind, and half the butter to the peach pulp and mash them together until well mixed.

4 Stuff the peaches with the filling and place in the greased dish. Dot with the remaining butter and dust with the cocoa powder and confectioners' sugar. Pour a little water into the base of the dish, place it in a preheated oven at 350°F, and bake for 30 minutes until golden. Serve with a dash of light cream.

54

RICOTTA PUDDING
DOLCE DI RICOTTA

The toasted slivered almonds in this recipe provide a contrast to the soft, creamy texture of the dessert.

SERVES 4

³/₄ cup almonds, slivered

3 egg yolks

2 cups Ricotta cheese

¹/₂ cup confectioners' sugar

¹/₃ cup Marsala wine

1¹/₄ cups whipping cream

1 Spread out the almonds in a foil-lined broiler pan and place under a moderately hot broiler until golden. Turn the almonds over frequently to prevent them from burning. Remove from the heat and leave to cool.

2 Beat the egg yolks with the Ricotta cheese, confectioners' sugar, and Marsala. Whip the cream until soft peaks form and fold it into the cheese mixture with two-thirds of the toasted almonds.

3 Spoon into serving glasses and decorate with the rest of the almonds. Serve chilled with *langues de chat* cookies.

Ricotta Pudding

FRUIT TARTS
CROSTATE

These fruit tarts are a real taste of summer. They can be as colorful as you like, depending on the fruits used to top the creamy custard filling.

SERVES ❹

12 oz sweet shortcrust pastry
(for 4 x 4 inch diameter tartlet pans)

1 egg, separated

1 egg yolk

$1/4$ cup superfine sugar

$1/3$ cup all-purpose flour

$1/3$ cup cornstarch

$1^1/4$ cups milk

1 tsp vanilla extract

8 oz soft fruits, such as
strawberries and raspberries

$1/3$ cup apricot preserve

---

1 Roll out the pastry and use to line 4 loose-bottomed 4 inch tartlet pans. Prick the bases with a fork, cover with foil to prevent them from burning, place in a preheated oven at 400°F, and bake for 15–20 minutes until golden and crisp. Remove the pans from the oven and set aside to cool.

2 Whisk the egg yolks and sugar until pale and thick. Sift in the flour and cornstarch, and mix to a smooth paste, adding a little milk if necessary.

3 Heat the rest of the milk until almost boiling and whisk into the paste. Return to the pan and stir over a low heat until the mixture boils, then remove from the heat.

4 Whisk the egg white until stiff and fold it into the custard. Return to the heat, stir in the vanilla extract, and cook for 2 minutes. Remove from the heat and leave to cool.

5 When the custard mixture is cool, use two thirds of it to fill the tartlets. Cover with the

fruit. Warm the apricot preserve
until it is runny and use it to
glaze the tarts.

Serve the remaining custard
on the side, or thin it with a little
cream and pour it over the tarts.

CREAM CHEESE AND RUM PUDDING
TIRAMISU

SERVES 8

6 tbsp rum

²/₃ cup strong black coffee

about 20 lady fingers

2 eggs, separated

2 cups Mascarpone cheese

¹/₂ cup confectioners' sugar

3 squares dark chocolate, grated

This is a very popular dessert found on almost every Italian menu. It is easy to make and can be prepared in advance and kept chilled.

1 Mix the rum with the coffee in a shallow bowl. Dip the lady fingers one by one in the liquid and lay them in a shallow dessert dish. Pour just enough of the remaining coffee and rum mixture over the lady fingers to moisten but not soak them.

2 Cream the egg yolks, Mascarpone cheese, and confectioners' sugar with the remaining coffee and rum.

3 Whisk the egg whites until they form soft peaks, then fold into the Mascarpone cheese mixture, and spread it over the lady fingers. Cover the top with the grated chocolate. If you like, you can also cover the top with sifted cocoa powder before adding the chocolate. Chill for several hours before serving.

CREAM CUSTARD

PANNA COTTA

This is similar to crème caramel, but without the caramel sauce. It is served chilled and is best when accompanied by a compôte of fresh or dried fruits.

SERVES ❹

1¹/₂ cups heavy cream

¹/₃ cup superfine sugar

1 tsp vanilla extract

1 tbsp brandy

2 tbsp water

1 tsp powdered gelatine

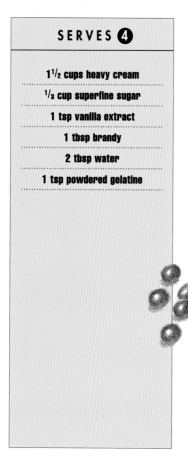

1 Put the cream and sugar in a pan and heat gently until the sugar dissolves. Add the vanilla extract and simmer for 3 minutes. Remove from the heat and stir in the brandy.

2 Pour the water into a heatproof bowl and sprinkle the gelatine on top. Stand the bowl in a pan of hot water over a low heat until the gelatine has dissolved. Whisk in the hot cream and remove from the heat.

3 Pour the custard into 4 individual ramekins, cool, and then chill until set.

Serve with fresh or dried fruits of your choice.

Cream Custard

INDEX